A Spectator

Ekphrastic Poetry

Per K. Brask

ΣKPHRΛSIS

Canada 2012

An **EKPHRASIS** Book

An imprint of **FICTIVE PRESS**
(a division of 2815699 Canada Inc.)

Copyright © 2012 by Per K. Brask.

Distributed in Canada and worldwide by lulu.com

"EKPHRASIS" and "FICTIVE PRESS" are trademarks of 2815699 Canada Inc.

Library and Archives Canada Cataloguing in Publication

Brask, Per K., 1952-

A spectator [electronic resource] : ekphrastic poetry / Per K. Brask.

Electronic monograph.

ISBN 978-0-9879170-8-9 (POD).

I. Title.

PS8553.R296S64 2012   C811'.54   C2012-901938-0

Cover design: FICTIVE PRESS

Front cover image: detail from "In the Theater" by Honoré Daumier, circa 1880. (Oil on canvas. Neue Pinakothek, Munich, Germany).

Back cover photo of author by Carol Matas.

Photographs accompanying poems by Per K. Brask.

Line drawing of Per K. Brask by Heather Spears: heatherspears.com/

To Carol, of course
and in memory of Inge Brask (1928-2010)

FOREWORD

*Spectatorship will always reveal more about
the spectator than the spectacle.*
John Freeman, "Autobiographical Spectatorship"

The Australian philosopher Paul Thom coined the term
"playing attention" to evoke the various levels at which
spectators during a performing arts event may be playfully
attending: between the performer's present actions, past
actions or anticipated ones; between performers; between
content and form; between this performance of a work
and previous ones; between the life on stage and personal
life and life "outside" the event. (See Paul Thom, *For an
Audience: A philosophy of the Performing Arts*, Temple UP,
1993, p. 205.)

Thus, each spectator puts together his own story, while
watching the performance, a story that doesn't only focus
on the performance currently attended, but a story that
draws together many aspects of the spectator's life in
general and the spectator makes up a meaning, perhaps,
from these various strands of experience. Or, as Jacques
Rancière appropriately says in his essay "The
Emancipated Spectator," this variegated activity suggests
that spectators put their own poems together. (See
Jacques Rancière, *The Emancipated Spectator*, Verso, 2009,
p. 13.)

Of course, spectating isn't an activity limited to attending performing arts events. Attending arts events in general, exhibitions and installations, puts some of us in the position of spectators, just as one may put oneself in the spectator position while observing events in daily life. Although most of the poems in this collection were written in response to theatrical performances, some are also responses to art exhibitions or life moments; they are all attempts to express the grasping for some meaning pursued by this one spectator's playful attention. That is, a spectator who (re)acts.

Per K. Brask

Let us open with a quote, a haiku from Monica Prendergast's prologue to her book *Teaching Spectatorship* (Cambria Press, 2008, p. xxi), a work I found vastly motivating:

> seeing performance
> an audience brings itself
> into new being

CONTENTS

SITTING THERE

sitting there as the lights go down before they come up
the show has begun. The unexpected will happen
even if you know the play. Its physical form
the voices, the bodies, the setting, they will all
be singular and different from when you read it
intonations, dialects, rhythms, cadences, ways
of walking you just couldn't have plumbed
in your reading mind, not to mention the cougher
in front or the man with cologne to the left
turning part of this into an inescapable olfactory event
(and the always present candy wrapper, of course)
often the seat will be uncomfortable, or you forgot
to hang your coat and toque in the lobby
then there's the forgotten shopping list
so no trip to Safeway after the show

Then:

this actor gets to you, and all care is about Hecuba
the distress and urgency is sharp and nuanced
you realize that though you've never worn her shoes
her agony pierces through the hope you'll never suffer a loss like hers
because no one should and only later when you are no longer held
does the argument you had at home seem petty as you head down
to Safeway to do the best you can without your list

MACBETH

at the Oregon Shakespeare Festival

I've always enjoyed reading *Macbeth*
but I've never seen a production I liked

until now

this actor, Peter Macon, performs Macbeth
like a hawk glides on an updraft

he lets the words and his character's will carry him
to places in the soul we'd rather not know about
but we let this actor take us there because

as Carol points out

this is, for all the blood spilt
and the corpses buried at the edge of the stage

this is a feminine interpretation

this Lady Macbeth, played by Robin Goodrin Nordli
is a woman seeking to become special, just a gal with a dream

not evil but misguided, who goes mad

when she realizes what she's done – and Macbeth loves her
and himself enough to catch the updraft when it arrives

hawks are predators after all no matter how decorative in the sky

these actors given air by this director, Gale Edwards, gave us cruelty
for love and now I doubt I'll ever understand the flight of a hawk in any
other way

UPON WATCHING HAMLET IN ASHLAND, OREGON

they got the wedding *kransekage* right
the cone shaped stack of marzipan-filled cake rings
with little Danish paper flags stuck into them
and, yes, some of those costumes you could see
on the streets of Elsinore today
(and I think I spotted the Danish
anti-nuclear power decal on his guitar case
when Laertes trundled off to France)

the players from the city formed
a hip-hop troupe and Hamlet himself
seemed, yes, (that word) seemed
in Dan Donohue's rendering
to be a rap-influenced white poet infatuated
with long vowels
(the things they learn down there in Wittenberg!)
perhaps to suggest to his mother that matter hints at mater
or just to make hip slant rhymes
leaving all nobility of mind behind from the start
so no loss when he died (it made sense that this Hamlet
would entrust his story to this doltish eternal student, Horatio
who'd seemingly no philosophy but to dress as a tramp)

he had to die this boy, we wanted him to die
this youth, this eternal youth (a *flab*
they might have called him in Danish, a rogue) who just did things
in mannered but by no means manly ways
there was no life in him, no animating principle
only the shell of behaviour

unlike Ophelia as rendered by Susannah Flood
an intelligent, self-possessed young woman
in a world where such possession cannot be had
(and so out of joint with Laertes and Polonius
but then no one gets to choose their family)
who was being forced so deeply into nothingness
that she had to drown herself in a halfhearted current
with stones in her pocket to ensure success

(Flood was the one to show us how
unconsoled despair may ruin more than a mind)

I half hoped she would pop up in some other dimension
(even as a ghost) where we could see a play about her
and maybe Claudius as rendered by Jeffrey King, a player
who also (in a better a better kind of seeming) seemed able
to make choices that portray the flow of the kinds of emotions
(in this case ambition's gushing well and the always
too late and useless regret) and views of the world a man like him
– or in the case of Flood's Ophelia – a young woman like her
could be living through. It is not a matter of what the actor feels
(though that may be a shortcut in preparation
with the caveat that in this tradition the job
of the actor is more to keenly observe
and reproduce than it is to self-express)
it is a matter of whether they can (also) portray
a persuasive possibility of such a person in such and such
a situation where such and such and such become
indistinguishable suches and we all – performers and audiences -
end up having our cake and eating it too

THOMAS OSTERMEIER'S HAMLET AT KRONBORG CASTLE

I sinned against one of Europe's theatre gods this evening
leaving his show halfway through and now I fear the consequences
what must I do to propitiate? To be seen as a connoisseur
who's best pleased when things are ambiguous. But the simple fact is
I was driven by boredom. I could no longer sit and attend to – not
nothing, there was all too much of something

I got my 345 Danish Kroner's worth though in the first few minutes
Hamlet's videography at the top projected onto a curtain of see-through
strands as he moved behind it and recorded himself and the five others
in character, followed by the funeral of old Hamlet when the gravedigger
in a Karl Valentin-esque routine ended up in the grave with the casket
while another actor provided bathetic rain via garden hose and Gertrude
waited for a scoopful of earth to throw in. These lazzi turned
the set's vast box of dirt into a sandbox for an evening of fun with death

that all stopped as we went to the drunken wedding reception
belching with bursts of hysterical histrionic rage
here contempt mixed with pleasure, that corroding
cocktail dissolvent of souls. But that was it. We never got further. The
rest was repetition. What Ostermeier seems to have seen
in the play is true and death may reasonably be preferred to being
under the influence of bullshot

by the time Ophelia with her little-girl voice entered to reveal
Hamlet's supposed secret love sickness I began my descent
down the bleachers and so from me the rest must be silence

THE BBC/RSC HAMLET ON DVD

the splendour of the RSC Hamlet as reframed by the BBC
is that David Tennant occupies the role in a state of anguish
he shows us from the beginning that his world is spinning
in a whorl of sorrow from his loss and disbelief in love
all trust gone that grace subtends the universe or that people
can be true. This impels Hamlet to seek the truth and Ophelia
to succumb when her scaffold of memorized ideals gives way
nothing will or can make sense to her – not even the meaning
of flowers. Claudius has driven all but lust for power from the land
and now pretense maintains the shine of a world order polished
to reflect back one's own desires – that and the fact that everyone
spies on everyone else – nothing else can stand as guide
until lies are swept away. But even the truth and honesty of a strongman
will not lead to a more desirable state and so the story must be told
and retold, reframed for how out of joint the time of our time happens to
be

JULIUS CAESAR
at the Oregon Shakespeare Festival

the cast worked well together
Vilma Silva thrived with her Caesar
and the director grasped her task
though Brutus destroyed the play

through no fault of his own

he just happened to be an able actor
in the wrong part (perhaps as Brutus
was an honest rebel in the wrong
conspiracy) his trucker gait (nothing
against truckers) and his tattooed arm
probably powerful in some other play
put this role beyond his reach

casting is *the* secret process, sometimes
conspiratorial, sometimes accidental, because
what seemed daring when talked through
and even still promising a week or two
later only reveals itself as a mistake
when it becomes clear that what played
like a newness, a surprising take in rehearsals
where everyone is in on the game
disappoints an audience who can't figure out
what on earth you were grasping at

CYRANO adapted by Frank Langella

University of Winnipeg Department of Theatre and Film

when all the players on the stage (taking turns)
play Cyrano, Cyrano becomes unstable, effeminate
at times and swashbuckling masculine (though not when played
by a male, ironically), tiny and curved, his large nose the only constant
constraint

then we in the audience also become Cyrano
sensing, remembering, knowing the beauty
that lies within our various uglinesses, whether hidden
or surrendered to each morning in the mirror, or happily for a moment
forgotten

and when Roxanne, too, comes in several voices
blonde and dark, wily and tough (though I hoped
that just once she'd appear in drag) then beauty turns out
not to be a single measure and perhaps we might all somehow be
partaking

the joy of performance covers hiccups of skill
and these students, guided by Skene, take us to a place where even death
is not an absolute end because stories keep moving into meaning
and watching is transformed into understanding that theatre is nothing
if not refracted love

JAKE'S GIFT

at Manitoba Theatre for Young People

it is two weeks before Remembrance Day and the flags
are accompanied by pipe playing "Highland Cathedral"

before the show
with its gift of three characters from one Julia Mackey
who shifts between their gestures voices and stances
sharp and quick delineations
the old Canadian veteran, Jake
a tremor in his left arm and grumpy resilience in his voice
the statuesque French grandmother
who teaches good manners
and the art of remembrance to her granddaughter
the curious and rambunctious Isabelle

simplicity is the name of the game
this is about actor and lights
that shape space and body
aura-like against black curtains

Jake's memory is personal
he fought along with his brothers and lost
one of them at Juno Beach

Isabelle is ten and is building memories
of her grandmother and now of Jake
her reach goes back before her birth
to when Grandmother was a girl of ten
named Isabelle who lost her father
to a Nazi bullet

this is also the Shabbat of Chaye Sarah
when we remember Sarah's life and Abraham's
buying her burial site and the new life he must enter
this is no one's memory but is remembered
as an act of culture – how we become identities

and this evening we become Canadians again
(because to take hold identity must be ever replayed)
with the help of an invented ten-year old French girl
on a nearly bare stage playing Juno Beach
paying our respects to those in whose deaths we live
as not American, not British, not French,
but as a different, blended pride
weather and geography play their part, too
we are reminded as we head into the first snow
glittering in the street lights

MUNGO PARK – THE MAN BEHIND THE NAME

Mungo Park, Kolding, visiting production at Mungo Park, Allerød, Denmark

on a Friday evening Allerød seems dead to the world
as my father and I seek out a place to eat before the show
we locate Cafésen in the centre of town and eat elaborate
starbursts (fried plaice with rémoulade, mayo, topped
with lemon, caviar and shrimp) though I'd rather have had
Shabbat dinner at home in Winnipeg with plain roasted
chicken and my special potatoes and listening to grandkids
singing the blessings. It's Shabbat Shelach where Moses
sends scouts (and spies) into Canaan to get the lay of the land
there are only six other people in the restaurant which is concerning
but the health inspector's certificate in the window shows a big smiley
and the starburst is tasty. We fear for the life of Allerød that this level
of tastiness attracts so few, but hope maybe they're used to better
and it turns out that they are because at the theatre there is a full house
and the show is alive with three male actors telling the us of Mungo Park
the Scottish explorer, often seen as a spy, who charted the course
of the Niger for Britain's Africa Association, and in the first act survived
through kindness and his insistence that negroes were human
and should be treated as individuals and in the second act discovered
that he was capable of animalistic barbarity, a good name for a theatre
that wants to engage us with the best and the worst of ourselves
facing all of life's shellacking

only Park is in something close to a historical costume while the other two
actors play all other parts in their street clothes, outfitted with wigs
and props according to need. The walls and floor of the stage are black
(like Africa as seen in the 18th Century) with a manually operated
turntable at centre stage. The black walls are soon covered with words
in chalk during the prologue where we are asked to imagine the story
told in a Hollywood movie with a phenomenal budget, opening
with a tracking shot over grass rippling in the wind on the Highlands

then taking a gut-dropping flight over a cliff rising from the ocean below
and there, there on the cliff a small figure climbs and "we" catch
our first glimpse of the daring young Mungo Park. And I do see that, just
like I see the boat he and his lieutenant steer through the second act
though it is, of course, just a stepladder lying on its side and their guns
are metal pipes. All is accompanied by a sometimes loud

soundscape with the bassy tones of Dolby Surround
it is a show built from exercises taught in most theatre schools
"here's a pencil, turn it into something else in a story so I can see it"
as audience you must be willing to fill the gaps.
They hint, you picture it in full. Unfortunately
my father prefers his theatre all dressed like the starburst
but I found myself enjoying a version of plain roasted chicken
(albeit superbly prepared and spiced by this crew)
with the added blessings provided by myself

DOVES

Picasso: Peace and Freedom
at Louisiana Museum of Modern Art, Denmark

when Louis Aragon picked *Colombe*
in 1949 for the poster of the *Congrès Mondial*
des Partisans de la Paix
he put the secular end to doves being doves
at least on paper or canvas

of Picasso's many doves my pick is the one
he drew on December 28, 1961. It was used
for the poster of the national congress
in May, 1962, at Issy-les-Moulineaux, titled
Colombe au rameau d'olivier

its simple undulating blue outline
and beaked green olive branch
may have taken him under a minute
but the time it takes to create is no measure
of the effect or quality of art

(though some like to give marks for effort)

and Aragon had the posters put up
the same day the image was picked

JASON AND THE ARGONAUTS

Visible Fictions Theatre from Scotland
at the Manitoba Theatre for Young People

they're really just boys playing those two men on the stage
men playing boys playing with their toy trunk, action figures
of the Argonauts (with Spiderman thrown in here and there)
and their huge wagon that turns into whatever is needed
like ship and jail cell and dragon's lair

yesterday's snowfall stayed thickly on the ground
and in the morning my granddaughter
of four threw herself into it and made angels
and at Shabbat dinner my grandson of six
having heard that ginger is good for you
wanted to have confirmed that this extended
to his gingerbread man he was having for dessert

Robert Jack and Tim Settle of Visible Fictions
excited us all kids and adults in the audience
embodying Bacchic pretense and letting go
into another world where you can be yourself
your friend, Jason and all the Argonauts
and Medea and Kings and servants and and and
and your friend can be all of those too
as long as you take turns and the story moves forward

and I went backward to my old backyard
with my teepee and its small fire place
and listening to Radio Luxembourg
on the transistor radio my father built for me
and going on dangerous scouting missions
in the fields behind our house
being prepared for new houses
with cavernous foundation holes
that could swallow you up and dissolve
you in their mud

just two of them there, Jack and Settle
on stage reminding us, showing us
that Dionysus can still hold us in his thrall
and when we let him have his due he will
fill us with awe and the sense that the possible
can be made visible right here right now

THE BORNHOLM REVUE
by Bornholm's Theatre at Rønne Theater, Denmark

"Learn wisdom from the show of life" is the guidance
imparted across the proscenium arch at Rønne Theater
(built in 1823) and that's what happens at this packed-to-the-rafters
revue as we laugh and snigger our way through skits and songs
that make us think back on the past year: Bornholm's near-catastrophic
encounter with snow and a miserably handled case
of fraudulent science; what happens when self-love psychology
goes bad and a person has to seek couple's therapy to regain trust
in herself; and Denmark's involvement in wars in Iraq and Afghanistan
the Vikings are back! Cathartic laughter. We are not superior to the jokes
we have been laughing at ourselves, this sure-footed cast makes it clear
we're in this together, their satire stings in scenes on the politics of daily
gossip ("not that it's any on my business") whether you're Bornholmer
or from off-island

my father who spent his national service on this Baltic island
(not long after the Russians had added many more ruins
to the ones left by the Germans) is in the best mood I've seen him
since my mother died last year. He and my mother took their last vacation
on Bornholm. Now he's getting weaker, though his cancer is growing
slowly, and his legs won't carry him sturdily. He has resisted
a walker till now, but recognizes coming down steep stairs
from the balcony and then walking to the car that the time
has possibly come and then we talk some more about gossiping
Bornholmers ("not that it's any of my business") whose dialect he loves
to imitate but can't – neither can I. His attempts, though, more than mine
make for the better show. Because he laughs in memory

AI WEIWEI

Louisiana Museum of Modern Art, Denmark

forty-two *Forever* bicycles made in Shanghai
welded together variously, right side up and up
side down and at angles form a circle of dense traffic
the handlebars are all missing, no steering required
when all must travel in the same direction, if they were
to move but the structure stands still and you are not
allowed to touch it or to spin tightly pumped tires
(as I clearly must have done) – the whole thing balances
in forced harmony. There's also the metal hanger
(the kind you get from the dry cleaner's) bent
into the profile of Duchamp and set in porcelain
(rhymes with *Fountain*). In the lower gallery are dried out hunks
of dead trees assembled into whole new ones and clusters of porcelain
rocks that from the balcony appear to rhyme with a Jean
Dubuffet sculpture until you look closer and see blue
rather than Jean's black edges and that Weiwei's pattern
rhymes with English china teacups, say, and so an enhanced edge
also becomes commentary

where Blake would say, "as a man is so he sees"
Weiwei says, "your own acts and behavior tell
the world who you are and what kind of society
you think it should be" and he demonstrates that
by using what he sees around him and casting
it in a new form as though the world could be turned
into one great ready(re)made where everything
can become more than what it is (dare I say repaired
and heightened?) and I want to believe that, too

SPAMALOT IN WINNIPEG

Broadway touring company at Centennial Concert Hall

on a day when the I Ching three times speaks
about oppression and the need to be cheerful
Monty Python's *Spamalot* comes to town
singing and whistling "Always look on
the bright side of life" even when it's shitty

and for two hours plus it's hard not to
get the message because this triple
A touring company is surely ready
for the big show. Their delivery is joy
through precision and timing

The Lady of the Lake, Arthur and crew
melt this already too wintery audience
and we are grateful and sunny
at intermission and later after the show
people leave whistling in the underpass

back to the parkade and no one gets irritated
at the bumper to bumper wait because time is
still rushing and lifting us above the cold
that also belongs to life. For a respite
Monty Python has aligned our perspective

with the Tao and the Stoics

THE SHUNNING

by Patrick Friesen at the Royal Manitoba Theatre Centre

I disobeyed, is the first line of the play
that brings us into the tailspin of a Mennonite
ostracized by his community for saying no
to a bit of doctrine

in the afternoon I'd been talking
with Bruce Sarbit about giving up
smoking and drinking
having to say no

so much of what you are
is a function of saying no
to your community
until of course they say no more

and in class talking about the mystery
plays like the Second Shepherds' Play
and the morality plays nailing their audiences
to paths of repentance

as Peter gets more isolated
the wall representing the church
encroaches evermore, pushing
everything to the edge

the importance of being
part of a world, to participate
and yet not merging, knowing you
as you, as a difference, to make a difference

Peter's brother has a defiant sense of humour
but stays in the fold. Peter's wife longs to have him back
but neither they nor Peter can find
a balance between no and yes

for us all whatever is chosen
the costs are dear

ALAN WILLIAMS

there were just the two of us in the rehearsal hall
Alan performing his trilogy "The Girl with Two Voices"
me listening to the story of his return to England
some fifteen or so years ago, listening to the events
and to his reactions, on two tracks, as it were

the hall in the basement of the UW
with its orange acoustic baffles is actually
a film studio so it was only appropriate
that Alan's description of Kew and Kew Gardens
projected fantasy versions on my inner screen

I hadn't seen Alan perform for many years
but had memories of him on stage in plays
and in earlier monologues like "The Cockroach
that Ate Cincinnati," memories of performance
that will never leave me

what he did in rehearsal of this new trilogy
was to pull me into an alpha state where his life
became my experience and the misery he recounted
reflected mine so that in effect he allowed himself
to become a mirror just by talking

just by sitting there and talking
sometimes struggling with a shoe lace
or pulling apart a muffin, sipping his coffee
allowing "it" to happen between us
in the way we used to fantasize

only live theatre could do

WATCHING JOE HAYES

at the Santa Fe Hotel

watching Joe Hayes conduct
tortillas out of the sky
in the hacienda of the Santa Fe Hotel

and to be bowled over by Shonto Begay
at the IAIA museum all in one day
gives an aura to this already enchanted place

where Georgia O'Keeffe, too, saw necessary ghosts
speaking through terracotta-red desert dirt
and adobe buildings crafted to complement its gift

IN THE NEXT ROOM

or The Vibrator Play *by Sarah Ruhl*
Royal Manitoba Theatre Centre, Warehouse

and, of course, the magic, who doesn't want to make angels
and love in the first snow and watch light dance in the flakes
coming, coming down slowly like some prayed for blessing
of a moment when the All comes together and you say, yes! yes!
or, oh God, or, something that rhymes with the sense of being alive
this is where differences disappear and the Tao clothes itself
in bodies to know what love is

it is what cannot be explained but can be simulated and then measured
as a current running through everything, unstoppable by convention
our complicated costumes revealed as just so much unnecessary invention

the final scene of does deliver a shade of this shared desire
weakly because most of the rest of the show was about jokey innuendo
repression and the cure for hysteria and surely, yes, the script holds that
except we already know that they were funny about sex back in the 1880s
even so their reach was no shorter than ours and even if it was harder
to get undressed and find each other in the dark, the dream of oneness
was known to them, though they went about it using other codes
more restricted than ours in some ways and more lyrical in others

and this too is held by the play if not by this production, the possibility
that we may understand them and us, each in our historical constraint
as well as our shared desire to become released

ALL OR NOTHING

by Bruce Sarbit
at the Winnipeg Fringe Festival

when Harry Nelken plays Miguel de Unamuno
in his cell after eleven weeks, each week presented
with a document to sign in support of Franco
he *performs* in the good old way. He uses to the full
his voice to modulate and to enlarge, to whisper
and to shift characters when Unamuno quotes. His stances
and gestures are often histrionic, angular and bombastic
– like the sculpture at Salamanca by Pablo Serrano –
forming the marriage of sensuality and Platonism
body and idea, that delivers flamenco, falangist
and anarchist, the allure of *duende*, life on the edge

Harry takes on Miguel's difficulties and delivers
his resistance to barbarism, his faith that renewal cannot happen
through death (creative destruction is a murderous delusion)
though it could mean that you'll have to die in the fight
against forces of Death, hoping to be remembered while risking
death swallowing all your traces. All that could be left is
a burning manuscript. The odds may be on the side of darkness
yet life must be played for all or nothing unless you want to settle
for nothing and not play at all

Harry's large Miguel gestures and big voice
calls to memory that, "If it is nothingness that awaits us
let us make an injustice of it; let us fight against destiny
even without hope of victory"

AT THE PALM SPRINGS ART MUSEUM

on the lower level there is a gallery of photos
of the American west. It is dark and you don't know
whether you're allowed in, but the lights go on when you enter
once there you could stand for hours in front of "Vanishing Race"
by Edward Sheriff Curtis, a foggy photogravure from 1904
a group of Navaho on horseback heading away
beside a trail leading to a large black shape, a mountain
their path surrounded by tall dessert plants and grasses
the one closest may be a woman with a baby on her back

upstairs in the main hall sits an "Old Couple on a Bench"
by Duane Hanson across from one of Chagall's "Village" murals
this one with a shochet, his hatchet raised for ritual slaughter
and in the Richard Avedon exhibit you get to remember
what Nureyev and the Factory people around Warhol looked like
and Groucho Marx as an old man, Marilyn Monroe as a sad girl
and happy with Arthur Miller – and Twiggy's face framed
by flowing hair. Vanishing, vanishing all is vanishing
some by murder, some because change, as per Heraclitus

is the only constant

MAYNARD DIXON'S TECHNIQUE

the sun reveals Dixon's technique
as it slides behind the San Jacinto Mountains

casting shallow beams through the pass
that fords the I-10 and onto the silvery foothills
below Joshua Tree

there it draws their separate folds
and veils each range like layers
of a riddle

it is hard not to imagine a boy
on his pony resting nearby

MACHINAL

by Sophie Treadwell
University of Winnipeg Department of Theatre and Film

sitting in the balcony
I am struck unnaturally
by the youth of this class
(or is it my age?)
many of whom I have taught or
am teaching in other
more bookish courses

they are keen this evening
to engage each other
a very good sign indeed
too often young actors
act in bubbles not paying
true attention to each other
or they take "thoughtful" pauses
when pace would make the audience think

but in this play about the machinery
of life, technologies and ritual
they respond to what they receive
more often than not they recover
quickly from mistakes
and still they show what
being caught in machinery
can look like
(in fact, skillfully recovering from a mistake
exposes the machinery of a show)

the more engaged they become
the clearer character caughtness is caught

ten women, one man in this class
some of the women nail a male
character with (e)razor wit

under Shelagh's direction Sophie's play speaks
perhaps louder than it did over eighty years ago

33

ROMEO, VAMPIRE-SLAYER

The Improvised Shakespeare Company of Chicago
at Manitoba Theatre for Young People

three players on an empty stage ask for suggestions
and take the first one heard and we're off
into a crazy world of Romeo the Vampire-slayer
in love with Julia the Vampire, born and bred
and a myriad of other characters including
three weird sisters to one of whom, Rosalind
Romeo had been promised in marriage
and a newly minted friar who turns out
to be Julia's long lost brother who in infancy
had been (experimentally) put in a basket and sent
downstream, (the experiment failed, he wasn't retrieved)
and raised by a friar in the woods (he never found
it peculiar that he never saw the sun or was fed
on rats, but then how could he have known any different?)
and so on till the end which I won't reveal
though the show will never be seen again
I'm glad and sad to say

Blanie Swen, Ross Braxton Bryant, Joseph Bland
took us on this silly and hilarious journey
in mock Shakespearean verse and prose sometimes
iambic blank verse, often rhyming couplets
with a verbal dexterity that must be envied
on any improv stage. So much fun was this Verona
that the near-blizzard (okay, I exaggerate a little)
was nearly forgotten in these riotous rhythms
young kids and older followed the rumpus
with eager eyes and ears, language and movement
the shifting of roles make Verona and its woods

and we, we want to know, we badly want to know
how it all turns out because we know that the players
also don't know, yet there is an inevitability at work
and they take us there to our surprise and we feel
grateful, so grateful that sheer silliness can give this much relief

TAKE CARE OF YOURSELF

when we arrive at the lower galleries
in Louisiana Museum of Modern Art
where Sophie Calle's "Take Care of Yourself" is installed
we first hear laughter, both recorded and live
because, as it turns out, people are laughing
at a clown, on a video screen, laughing as she reads out loud
and comments on the use of brackets and ellipses
in the e-mail Sophie Calle had received from her boyfriend
telling her that he's dumping her because he can't live
up to his promise of only seeing her and not
his other three lovers. Those French, you say, and think of Sartre
and all his women. But unlike "The Beaver," Sophie Calle did not want
to be number four and besides she found the e-mail puzzling so she asked
107 women to interpret it, each from her professional standpoint
hence the clown, the actress, the Indian dancer, the singers, the ballerina
the literary critic's commentary, the composer's score. 107 responses
to a highly intellectual dear Joan letter ending with pleasantly good advice
"Take Care of Yourself." So she did, by all those women telling him off
did he not realize that the artist he had been dating for months loves
texts and images, loves to mix intimate with public?
did he desire her hilarious revenge? No, his letter may be devious
but he shows no sign of brilliance

an exhibit crowded with couples whispering to each other,
girlfriends chuckling, and kids and their parents laughing
is a good place to be. Even my father who's not generally a friend
of modern art smiles at the parrot on the screen who' s learnt to say
"Take Care of Yourself." We've come because my mother died
a few days ago and she enjoyed this place. We've been here
almost every time I've been back for a visit – for art, coffee
and pastry in all sorts of weather. This is a day she would have loved
a calm sea and a clear view of Sweden across the sound

leaving the Sophie Calle exhibit we pass her memorial to her mother
"souci," her mother's last word, repeated on consecutive glass
plates leading to a photo of her on her death bed. My mother
also said that she was worried, nervous just before she died and
had we entered there rather than exited, we would not have seen
"Take Care of Yourself"

THREE SISTERS ADAPTED BY BRUCE MCMANUS

Theatre Projects Manitoba presenting Zone 41

Theatre Projects Manitoba presenting Zone 41
what was gained by moving the play close to an airbase
at Moose Jaw, Saskatchewan in the 1950s? What was gained
but the "spectacular" jet flight exhibition cum dog fight
that it took us almost three hours to get to? What was gained
was moments in McManus's dialogue that sounded right
coming from this cast. No phony Russianness was our relief

this Three Sisters, played out on an alley stage, too often
left you in the dark as your gaze was brutally
shifted from one end of the stage to the other, manhandled
by the lighting plot or because you couldn't see, though others could
what was happening among the clump of actors down in the left court
while you maintained a clear view of audience members siting across

most relationships faltered as they will and must in Chekhov
but here everyone seemed to live in bubbles from the very top
nothing was broken up because everything had already burst
except in the case of the doctor, played by Harry Nelken
who showed us a man no longer able to exist on nostalgic fumes
his plane spiraling out and he's not even reaching for a parachute

he became the centre of the show because here choices were made
that drew attention and the story was told that life both is and is not
in our desires' control

THIS STONE HAS LEGS

it's found its way from Palm Desert
and it's been rummaging around
first in a leather pouch
then in a homemade (decorative) ashtray
ever since the mid-nineties of the last century
when I "rediscovered" it today
I could swear I heard my own steps on desert sand

TIME ENCROACHES

and sits there
as flowers wilt
and I try to retain
as much as I can
of Chekhov's *Three Sisters*

projecting what I have to say
into the future
I expect
with the same trust
I extend
to Chekhov's past
and the flowers on his mantelpiece

IT'S A LONG HAUL

to get to almost
nowhere; there's
a by-pass, so you
could avoid us. But
if you do head through
our town take some
time to acclimatize.
It's not that I'm
embarrassed about
our town – though I
used to be. It's just
that outsiders find it
really ugly – and it is.
It's a prairie city, after
all. Those of us who've
lived here for decades
still notice that it's a
far cry from a place
you'd love to come
from and yet we've
adapted; we know
some of the reasons
why we're here,
why we have to be
here. Maybe if you
stay a little while,
take in a show,
have a meal,
a sleepover,
talk to us,
you'll get a sense
of what we see,
though neither
we nor you
will ever see
what those who've
always been here
can see.

BLUE

I'm writing with a blue pencil because I've become a royalist
(a Danish royalist). It came upon me in just 6 days. I arrived on Saturday
and this very afternoon —viewing an exhibition at Frederiksborg Castle
about queen Margrethe II who turns 70 tomorrow — I became a royalist

Tuesday and Wednesday evening Danish TV was dedicated to the queen
and I watched with fascination — surprising myself
(after all I haven't lived here for 35 years)
I even discovered a clichéd lump in my throat

my father is tired of the queen. He makes fun of her verbal mannerisms
imitating them – quite well, if truth be told
"It's time for her to step down," he says, "retire already"
he's not a republican. He wants her son Frederik to become king

there's a great painting of Frederik's wife, Mary, in the exhibition
where my royalism was clinched. It shows the crown princess
putting on a glove of a pair that symbolizes (it said) the obligations
she's taken on as Denmark's future queen.

though she's standing in the garden room at Fredensborg Castle
(the royal summer residence) the mirrors behind her reflect buildings
from her home town of Hobarth in Tasmania. She's a Dane (now)
and quite hip and I'm a prairie boy (now) headed for retirement,

images of a Danish queen
reflected in non-existing mirrors behind me

WHITE

I'm writing with a white pencil (on the black inside cover of my note pad)
because there's a Buddha sitting on the lawn of a farm house
just as you enter the tiniest of villages, Koster, on the island of Møn

at first it looks out of place until you remember
that a Nobel-Prize winning German novelist has a home on the island
that its light, so clear on this spring day, has beckoned a bundle of artists

(I remember from school that artists come in schools – but so do fish
and the fisheries around here aren't doing as well as the artists these days)

the butt of the island where it juts the furthest into the Baltic Sea
tells its 70 million year-old story, displaying a chalky grin
not unlike that exhibited by the more celebrated artist at Dover

PINK

I'm writing with a pink pencil
because I'm finally on a plane
on my way back to Winnipeg
and the attendant has just given me a can
of sparkling water

The hospital my mother was in
the past few days was gray concrete
on the outside and on the inside
an assortment of candy, designed
by the late artist Poul Gernes
(whose daughter is a poet)
in the late 60s, early 70s. His idea was
that sparkly hospital walls would enhance healing
things there are pretty run down now
but I'm hoping for the best

Louisiana, the museum of modern art
north of Copenhagen, is running an exhibition
on Colour in Art, including Kandinsky
Nolde, Matisse, Miro, Picasso…
not to forget a couple of Calder's mobiles
because there's a balance that must be heeded
between something there and something gone
and in how this airplane stays aloft

BLUES

some blues singer wails about shame
on the local NPR station as we hurtle along the stream of red lights
on the San Bernadino Freeway
"you oughta be ashamed" but I don't listen to the reason
because my mind is completely taken over by images
from the Autry Museum of Western Heritage
my new Jerusalem
where they celebrate the singing cowboy and the artists
of personality who met themselves on their way through
the desert's pink and purple landscapes

I do like the blues. I have since my father gave me the first Stones album
when I was 12 on a rainy day in Odense, Denmark
even then those stories shot at the Iverson Ranch
in the Santa Susanna Mountains
had long stoked my longing
and now having just seen the picture of Charles Strauss
mayor of Tucson in 1883 posing with his son and looking
to all the world like a guy who knows what's what
I get the feeling that a day-dreaming kid from the old country
now Canadian
a Jew by choice
has a chance if he dares come out in the noonday dust
and face himself in the sun
without shame

THE WISDOM OF THE SMALL

from the olive tree at the sidewalk
a Costa's Hummingbird (*Calypte costae*)
descends over the terrace to check me out

he hovers slightly above my eyes
just out of reach. I check him
out, too, his purple gorget shining

his wings vibrating. He backs up
I carry no nectar, but he stays
watching me watching, making peace

perhaps, or asking if I know the way
to God? "I do," I tell him, "from looking
at you." He tinkles his high notes

satisfied, I hope, with our exchange
then he disappears around the corner
looking for his favorite red penstemon

he knows the business of his life
as I would like to know mine

AN UNKINDNESS OF RAVENS
especially for Carol

Chihauhuan Ravens surf a vortex of wind
above the city
a silent pledge of change

celebrating flight

because they can and right now
no other desire or need matters more
than being together – flying

and us watching

ONE MORE MILE

on Wednesday evenings John Koonce and One More Mile
play the Rock Creek Tavern somewhere outside Portland
and everyone (from my two year-old granddaughter to her
eighty-one year-old great-grandfather) gets into the groove
of some old-fashioned rock and country along with a menu
of burgers and fries, salads and soups, home crafted beer and wine

the band's two groupies start the dancing – probably wives of members
John Koonce, well past fifty for sure, needs knee replacements
but his guitar riffs during the instrumental opening – "Walk, don't Run" –
fly off his strings

there are a few what you might call mistakes of beat and phrasing
but that makes the whole vibe all the better in this down home joint
built in timber in 1973 by (photos show) hippies with enough savvy
to keep it groovy now for over forty years. Time obviously likes to replay
its best tunes in spots you'd least expect

THE MUSIC MAN
at the Oregon Shakespeare Festival

after watching a performance of *The Music Man*
we are drawn towards a drumming circle at the Plaza
in Ashland where an organizer for the Second Chance Scholarship tells us
when we ask that a number of first nations used to traverse the Siskiyou
but that they were removed from this area. The Talcomah and the Shasta
I think he said were the most frequently resident. Removed, I thought
to make room for Shakespeare and musicals

The Music Man enjoyed colourblind casting with white, black, Asian
as well as signing performers. But there were no American Indians
in this Iowa burg. Only the fake band created by the mayor's wife,
an awkward recollection within earshot of the drum

THE LANGUAGE ARCHIVE by Julia Cho

at the Oregon Shakespeare Festival

that a single line at the end of a show
can turn an experience of perfect charm
into a disappointment is quite unexpected
but when we learn that George never fell in love
with Emma, it is quite unacceptable
because that's exactly what we been watching
happening between this George and this Emma

so maybe Cho needs two options for the end
one in which we're told that they lived happily together
with ups and downs and huge fights in Esperanto
along with a myriad of kids because we hunger
to be told that and it's just mean to withhold
from us what we want out of fear of seeming
sentimental

and another, the one we got, where George never
falls for Emma, so that each production gets
to choose what works best for the actors at hand
because in this case it is simply not possible
not to fall in love with Susannah Flood

WÖLFLI'S ASYLUM

is that Doufi, the child of poor and depraved parents,
riding the dark horses? Or, is it St Adolf the Second?
but there, surely, that's Wölfli peaking up from below the fire!

when the whirling pictures simply won't stop there's nothing left
but to reach for the golden promises that lie whispering,
"listen up, for I am guiding you through the darkness
Orpheus has been waiting for you since your earliest breath"
yet, we never get there because of the spurs stabbing
ever deeper into the soul's ribcage urging, urging
on the horses of schizophrenia and depression

there'll be no redemption, what's done is done
and it will haunt you till you own it freely
with yes, yes I did that, the terrible deed was mine
no amount of crowding out the canvas with figures
and words can hide the terror of a blank piece of paper
it is not what you did that made you unreal, unfree, Wölfli
it was your escape into Waldau Clinic. Yes, yes, yes!
your art was good. But the struggle, the struggle simply is
not about them against us and it cannot be settled
by galloping into fantasy. Let's share instead
a steaming bowl of *Campbell's Tomato Soup* and contemplate
the pitch of the *Asylum Band*, or the *General View of the Island
of Neveranger* with its criss-crossing snakes and ladders
the faces and the scattered eyes and the goat's head
you put there to warn us that living like Janus is both dangerous
and necessary. We must, you say, both see the mutilated child
and hear the music of the spheres, without creating contempt
for the world, or sending out a posse of personalities
in search of Messiahs

and, so, it is now proclaimed that Doufi the child
and St Adolf the Second – and the horses
are all one and the same; that we each carry our freedom within
and yet we do not

TRANSLATORS MEET AT UNDERWOOD

sometimes an alchemical process doesn't take much
you can, for instance, turn an old neighbourhood tavern
into a literary events place offering books, food and drink
and call it *Underwood* in reverence of that iconic typewriter
as they've done at Nørrebro in Copenhagen

and then you can invite a group of translators to read
in English and in Danish and get a feel for the changes
and sameness that make something new out of something already there
which is, granted, not as surprising as something out of nothing
but it does make travel between languages possible

and then as these translators read their translations
you will sense shifts in personality as they wear the masks
of other writers in new form. Their own writing is different
but they enjoy the ruse of attempting to ring true
in another's voice as they rejoice in the *Ecotone* happiness issue
and convey an American journal to Copenhagen

READING MICHEL HENRY INTO SASKATOON

the trees along the river walk
on the banks of the South Saskatchewan
are striving towards pistachio green
in an attempt to calm the (nearly too) bright
morning light.

things stand out in sharp relief
on such a morning, explaining (perhaps)
why so many artists live around here:
shapes and colours pronounce the measures
of the world

as though they were life
which like love is not an object but itself
lived as when (nearly) pistachio green leaves
share (the pathos of) life's flow
with me

ADRIAN STIMSON: *BEYOND REDEMPTION*

Mendel Art Gallery, Saskatoon

the stuffed bison
surrounded by little bison
pelts supported by wood frames
and the paintings of nuclear explosions
behind a bison standing
in a prairie winter landscape
and the video of a white one, *Natoyiini*
a Holy Buffalo to the Blackfoot

the quiet of the room
with just the two of us
forced to contemplate
violent disappearance
and whether we are all
beyond redemption
(for every continent
has lived its trauma)

but back outside
on the river walk
in the sunshine
with the crazy sounds
of active water birds
and later in the Souleio bistro
with Panini and tea
something like redemption
seems possible again
(remembering and forgetting
must go hand in hand)

SOPHIE TAEUBER-ARP & CO

standing in front of a cast
of marionettes once intended
for a production of Gozzi's
König Hirsch, Il re cervo
or The King Stag, created
in 1918 by Sophie Taeuber-
Arp with Dada flair
you may realize in a rush
that experiments in life
inevitably perish
no one's pulling
those particular strings
any longer and you know
from the video playing
next to the installation
that remounting it is ghostly
work. It's gone with all the rest
and yet we also know
in the same instant
that without women
like Sophie Taeuber-Arp
or Hannah Höch
and her puppets, or
someone like Claude
Cahun and her
photographic self-portraits
playing with gender
as a Buddha, a weight lifter
androgynous boy, Barbe Bleue
or in a robe with masks
without women like Sophie
Taeuber-Arp or Hannah Höch
or Calude Cahun,
there'd be fewer questions
to ask now and
we might have been more
ghostly today

FEAST
Winnipeg Art Gallery

it's minus twenty-seven in Winnipeg
but I have some time before meeting Claire for coffee
at Stella's eatery so I go to see the exhibit Feast
at the WAG which turns out not to be quite so feasty

there are vessels and spoons and paintings
of carrots and bags of onion
the merriment Kertész caught in his print
of a celebration in Montparnasse
after the first futurist ballet with people
raising glasses and laughing, exactly
the kind of rambunctious joy opening nights call for
and Kelly Clark's photo montage of the debris
after a dinner "with George," and the sweet row
of women seniors gathered with tea, coffee, sandwiches
and serviettes and the curves, the curves of the Russell Wright
dinner service recall the industrial attempt at ritual

but as lovely as this is and as much as it brings back memories
of great dinner parties my parents hosted conjuring horns
of plenty and laughter deep into the night before I was asked
to chauffeur folks home again – and the parties we, Carol and I
used to throw until we decided we partied best alone
those memories surpass the show. So I walk to Stella's
in crunching snow and air that could freeze your lungs

to talk with Claire over coffee and grilled cinnamon buns
that become the real feast of this afternoon

AFTER READING VAN GOGH

by Naifeh and Smith

the spectacle that emerges
yet again is of the artist as asshole
self-absorbed, mooching, fornicating
self-justifying, cruel, ungrateful and single minded
in these respects Naifeh's and Smith's van Gogh
resembles their earlier Pollock
and makes for another dispiriting read
instance piles on instance of bad behavior
fabricating the sense that if you want to become a genius
start by making grief for others
let your demons spew their muck because in the end
you'll serve humankind by creating the new

I don't actually understand van Gogh's paintings
better now and I certainly don't understand genius
unless it's implied that you need dirt to grow irises
but if that is so why not follow Otto Rank
and turn inward and create a compassionate character
rather than pretty paintings – or whatever else?
yes, we need both genius and love
but I refuse to believe that they cannot exist
in the same person

PREPARING TO WRITE

preparing to write an essay
on O'Neill's *A Touch of the Poet*, again
the trip we took to Tao House all
those years ago comes back in flashes
of the room, like a captain's cabin
where he wrote, and the female park ranger
reading from *A Long Day's Journey Into Night*
the view of Diablo's peak through the window
and his tiny script, barely legible
that shaped his ambitious world

there was something of the sea
in those hills around Danville
befitting his history and his longing
like so many he destroyed himself
forever wanting more than could be
given by anyone, not even by the world
yet he gave more than should be asked
though it always is: the artist must
give us all or the world feels cheated – a price
for making what no one knew they needed

THE WRONG KIND OF SNOW by Alan Williams

in Krista Jackson's living-room, Winnipeg

in Krista Jackson's living-room, Winnipeg
sitting on a stool against a wall and sometimes leaning forward
on the kitchen counter Alan Williams recounts his return
to England in 1996 after fifteen years in Canada, reconnecting
with new old roots in London, (because he's from Manchester
but lived in London for a while in the 1970s) relearning the codes
via, first, classifications of types – typically English, London, Manchester
and eventually to being mentally back to where things are what they are

gathered in Krista Jackson's house are thirty or so members
of the Winnipeg theatre community, many who knew Alan
when he lived here, many he taught, and many who know him
by the reputation he left behind of an actor, a writer and a director
of shows worth attending. That's why they are here tonight, some
foregoing the Grey Cup game on TV, the Blue Bombers against the Lions
(as it turns out Winnipeg lost, but we who gathered at Krista's won)

watching the many in this group who are so used to being watched
and therefore know what good watching entails was like being let in
from the cold. It wasn't about inside jokes, it was about keen sensitivity
to inflection and dialect, the way a soul reveals itself in breath and rhythm
authenticity is both real because it just is and it is also performed
but it is never put on. Constructed and thought out, yes, and
even if it takes some strategy, authenticity is never strategized

you learn that when you watch a superb performance along with actors
who just watch and listen and the good snow has arrived outside

LARS von TRIER

in the modern collection at Frederiksborg Castle
there's a self-portrait of Lars von Trier from 1975
when he was nineteen, four years before he entered
film school. The portrait is, of course, amateurish

it shows a young man peering with blue eyes
at the spectator. His black hair is slicked back
a thin strand falling across his right eye and a long drop
of blood pours from the corner of his mouth

a black cloud surrounds him, a blue sky is suggested in the upper
left corner and in the lower right corner three crosses stand
next to each other on a hill silhouetted by the site of an explosion
(David Caspar Friedrich meets Vasily Vereshchagin in negative space)

"On the way to Zarathustra"

is the title. A young man's Nietzschean dream of himself
as the new human, the Übermensch, the one to survive the overthrow
of the gods and recreate himself and his world in his own image?
it would explain a lot – if a life were that simple

RUD. RASMUSSEN'S SHOWROOM

Niels took me to see the Rud. Rasmussen showroom
at Nørrebro in Copenhagen and I fell in love with a desk
designed by H.J. Wegner in 1955. Just a rectangular desk
crafted in oak. Its lines were so clean, quiet and, well, seductive

a person could write fanciful things at that desk, sitting, perhaps
in a chair also designed by Wegner, like his chair from 1949
with a woven seat, the chair he called "the round one" (with leather
seats it was used in the Nixon-Kennedy TV debates) imagine

being able to put new drafts into each of the three drawers
right below the desktop after reading them under the light
from a Kaare Klint lamp mounted on the wall and as you move
to put a draft into the drawer your wrist caresses the wood

across the room I'd want a Kaare Klint three-seater sofa
designed in 1935 in European cherry and ox hide, so I could sit
or lie down, stretched out, and look over at the Wegner desk
and imagine what could be written by someone sitting there

NOT THIS TIME, EITHER
(Or, How the Spectator Misses a Show)

so for the second time
in ten days we chose
to stay home and not go
to the movie theatre
(though we did have the time)
to see *Pina* despite the fact
that I ought to have gone
at least once. After all
Bausch invented the ways
of making dance theatre

the first time
we were exhausted
so watching Beckett
and Castle on the home
screen (recorded, speeding
through commercials)
solving murders and not
declaring their love
seemed more seductive

and the second time
you were working out
a problem in your book
so we talked a little
about Parashat Yitro
the ten commandments
and how the Jews became
a holy nation. That seemed
a much better use
of time

THEATRE COUNTS

an afterword of sorts by way of a found poem
plucked from Alain Badiou's observations in **Rhapsody for the Theatre** *

theatre counts on the spectator
does not take place without spectators

The Spectator: Point of the real
by which a spectacle comes into being

Theatre demands that its spectator […] attach
the development of meaning to the lacunae of the play,
and [..] become […] the interpreter of the interpretation

A representation is […] the inquiry into the truth
of which the spectator is the vanishing subject

there is something painful in the attention
[…] required from the spectator
He is summoned, not to experience pleasure […] but to think

[The] encounter functions for the spectator as an elucidation of the present
the real function of theatre consists in orienting us in time,
in telling us where we are in history

Nothing can ever make up for, or excuse, not having been a Spectator
theatre counts on the spectator

* in *Theatre Survey* 49:2 (November 2008), translated by Bruno Bosteels

ACKNOWLEDGEMENTS

I feel deeply grateful to my wife, Carol Matas, for a vast number of things, one of them being her careful editing of my work.

To the poets Patrick Friesen and Niels Hav, and, fellow traveler into investigating spectatorship, Claire Borody, who have all given helpful responses to many of the poems in this collection; my Chair, Tim Babcock, and my colleagues in the Department of Theatre and Film at the University of Winnipeg, as well as Dean David Fitzpatrick, Acting Dean Glenn Moulaison and VP (Academic) John Corlett who made possible my Leave so I could get this collection into shape; Daniel Meyer-Dinkgräfe of the University of Lincoln, UK, for publishing much of my recent creative writing in *Consciousness, Literature and the Arts*; Bent Holm of the University of Copenhagen for the many years of good discussions on and work together in the theatre; Morri Mostow and Doug Long of FICTIVE PRESS for publishing this collection—many, many thanks.

PER BRASK ON EKPHRASTIC EXPRESSION

"Ekphrasis"—a literary description of or commentary on a work of art.

(http://www.merriam-webster.com/dictionary/ekphrasis)

What attracts me to ekphrastic expression is that I like to watch and observe. It also allows me to combine my love of theatre and other art forms with my love of poetry. By writing about my personal reactions to a performance or an artistic work, I hope to move beyond what a reviewer normally does, which is to assess, to give a sense of how it was experienced, if only by me. And, for me, the best way to record such an experience is in poetic form.

I particularly like poetry that attempts to understand a work of art, a concrete experience, a person, an event, an object. One of my favourite poets is Frank O'Hara. Many of his poems written during his lunchtimes in New York are reflections on his artist friends, on observed events or his response to what he saw around him. Among his narrowly ekphrastic poems, I recommend "On seeing Larry Rivers' 'Washington Crossing the Delaware' at the Museum of Modern Art." Other ekphrastic poems I value highly are W.H. Auden's "Musée des Beaux Arts" and Philip Levine's "M. Degas teaches art and science at Durfee Intermediate School, Detroit, 1942." In other words, my preference is for poems that are about something and that leave the reader with something to think about, some—big or small—life issue. Preferably written in fairly direct language, what the poet Harry Youtt calls "plain speech poetry."

A Spectator is my first published collection of ekphrastic poetry.

ABOUT PER K. BRASK

Per K. Brask is an accomplished dramaturg and author who has published poetry, plays, short stories, essays and literary translations.

Since 1982, Per Brask has taught acting, playwriting, directing, theatre aesthetics and play analysis in the Department of Theatre and Film at the University of Winnipeg (Canada) and was appointed Visiting Professor in Theatre and Consciousness at the University of Lincoln (UK) for a three-year term in January 2010. Prior to this, he was dramaturg for Playwrights Workshop and Artistic Director of the Saidye Bronfman Centre Theatre, both in Montreal (Canada). During his time in Montreal, he also taught playwriting at Concordia University and at the National Theatre School of Canada. Throughout his career he has acted as dramaturg on numerous plays and productions.

He has published poetry, short stories, translations, interviews and essays in such journals as *Anthropologica, Border Crossings, Canadian Folklore, Canadian Theatre Review, C.G. Jung Page, Contemporary Verse 2, Consciousness, Literature and the Arts* (on whose editorial board he serves), *Danish Literary Magazine, Descant, Event, Grain, Journal of Dramatic Theory and Criticism, The Literary Review, Malahat Review, Modern International Drama, NeWest Review, Nexus, Performing Arts Journal, Poetica, Poetry Canada Review, Poet Magazine, Prairie Fire, The Philosophers' Magazine* and *Zygote.*

He has written several radio dramas for CBC Manitoba and he has written plays and libretti, including the libretto for Michael Matthews's chamber opera *Prince Kaspar*.

Brask's books include *Power/lessness* (monologues, Turnstone Chapbooks,1987), *Duets* (short stories, with George Szanto, Coteau, 1989), *DramaContemporary: Scandinavia* (plays, ed., PAJ, 1989), *Double Danish* (short stories, ed. and trans., Cormorant, 1991), *Aboriginal Voices: Amerindian, Inuit and Sami Theatre* (essays, plays and interviews, ed. with William Morgan, Johns Hopkins UP, 1992), *God's Blue Morris: A Selection of Poems* by Niels Hav (ed. and trans. with Patrick Friesen, Crane Editions, 1993), *Contemporary Issues in Canadian Theatre and Drama* (essays, ed. Blizzard Publishing, 1995), *Essays on Kushner's Angels* (ed. Blizzard Publishing, 1995), *The Woods by Klaus Høeck* (poems, trans. with Patrick Friesen, Crane Editions, 1998), *Seven Canons* (plays by Canadian women ed. with Martin Bragg and Roy Surrette, Playwrights Canada Press, 2000), *Two Plays by Ulla Ryum* (trans. Adler & Ringe, 2001), *A Sudden Sky: Selected poems by Ulrikka S. Gernes* (ed. and trans. with Patrick Friesen, Brick Books, 2001), *We Are Here* a collection of poems by Niels Hav (ed. and trans. with Patrick Friesen, Book Thug, 2006), and *Copenhagen* a collection of short stories by Katrine Marie Guldager (trans., Book Thug, 2009), *Performing Consciousness* (ed. with Daniel Meyer-Dinkgräfe, Cambridge Scholars Publishing, 2010).

Edited and Co-Edited Books:

http://www.alibris.com/search/books/author/Brask,%20Per, %20Professor/aid/618254

http://www.c-s-p.org/Flyers/Performing-Consciousness1-4438-1634-5.htm

Creative Writing:

In *Consciousness Literature and the Arts* (various pieces):
http://blackboard.lincoln.ac.uk/bbcswebdav/users/dmeyerdinkgra
fe/archive/archive_creative.html

In *Canadian Journal of Practice-based Research in Theatre* (Vol.3, No.1:
"Seeing Shakespeare" a suite of poems):
http://cjprt.uwinnipeg.ca/index.php/cjprt/article/viewFile/32/21.

Literary Translation:

We Are Here by Niels Hav (co-translated with Patrick Friesen)
http://www.bookthug.ca/proddetail.php?prod=2427

Copenhagen by Katrine Marie Guldager
http://www.bookthug.ca/proddetail.php?prod=200914

A Sudden Sky by Ulrikka S. Gernes (co-translated with Patrick
Friesen)
http://www.brickbooks.ca/?page_id=5&authorid=42